Easy Gosp Songbook for Piano

Book with Audio Access

By
Lee Davis

Free Online Audio Access
Go to this address on the internet:

cvls.com/extras/egsp/

About This Book

This songbook features beginning to intermediate arrangements for classic gospel songs. The first arrangement you will learn for each song features interesting and recognizable melodies using mainly the right hand along with basic left hand parts. The last section of the book displays each song along with chord progressions, lyrics, and vocal melody lines. This is a great setup for sing-alongs because the lyrics are written in a large font so that multiple singers and musicians can read along.

Audio Tracks

This course also includes access to audio tracks to help you learn and practice. We have included three different recordings of each song. The first version features just the piano playing the melody line. The second version has the piano playing along with other instruments. The last recording features the other instruments with no piano so that you can practice playing the piano part in context.

You may access these files by going to the following web address:

cvls.com/extras/egsp/

The Author

Lee Davis is an Atlanta session musician and performer with over 20 years of experience playing and teaching piano. Lee performs nightly with some of the top acts in the South. He also does extensive recording work with MLD Productions and Maysville Music, and has recorded two solo CDs.

Watch & Learn Products Really Work

30 years ago, Watch & Learn revolutionized music instructional courses by developing well thought out, step-by-step instructional methods that were tested for effectiveness on beginners before publication. These products, which have dramatically improved the understanding and success of beginning students, have evolved into the Watch & Learn system that continues to set the standard of music instruction today. This has resulted in sales of more than three million products since 1979. This easy to understand course will significantly increase your success and enjoyment while playing the piano.

Table of Contents

The Songs

The Songs with Lyrics

Learning the Keys

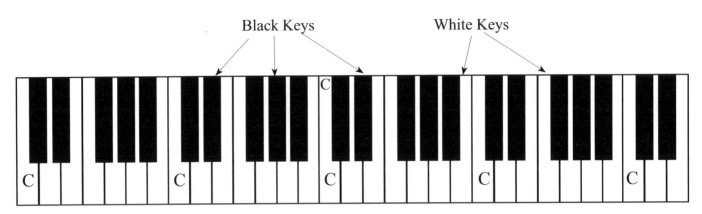

Pianos have 88 keys. Electronic keyboards usually have less. You may have 76, 61 or fewer.

The White Keys

The keys are divided into black and white keys. Black keys are divided into groups of twos and threes. The most important key for locating your place on the keyboard is middle C. The note C is always located directly left of the group of 2 black keys. Middle C is the C closest to the center of the keyboard.

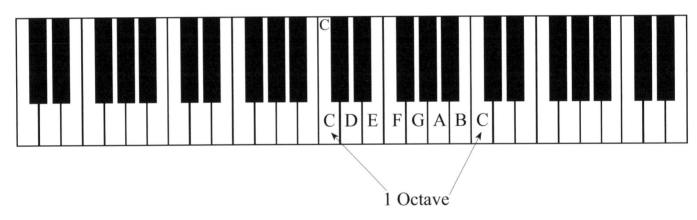

Starting with middle C, the white keys are: C-D-E-F-G-A-B-C

Once you reach C again, it is an octave higher. An octave is a group of 8 notes from one C to the next C. The notes are named in this manner up and down the keyboard. Up the keyboard is to the right. Down the keyboard is to the left.

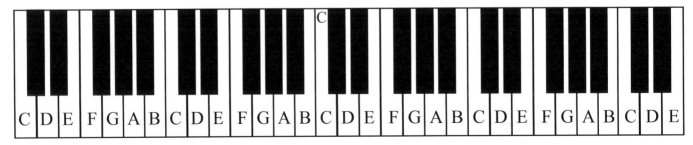

The Black Keys

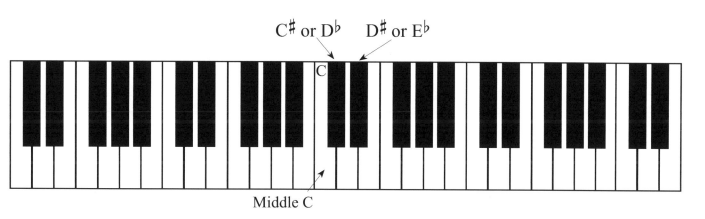

Notice that the black keys are grouped in twos and threes all the way up and down the keyboard. Find middle C again. Just to the right of middle C is the black key C sharp. Sharp means one key higher than the original note. This same black key could also be called D flat. Flat means one key lower than the original note. The black keys to the right of middle C are C sharp or D flat, D sharp or E flat.

♯ Symbol means sharp, or 1 key to the right
♭ Symbol means flat, or 1 key to the left

The group of three black keys are as follows: F sharp or G flat, G sharp or A flat, A sharp or B flat. Remember, each black key has two names, one using a sharp and the other a flat. Sharp means one key or half step higher than the white key to the left. Flat means one key or half step lower than the white key to the right.

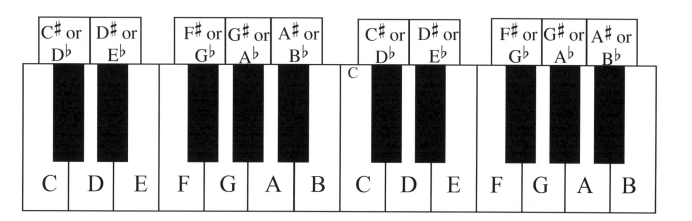

The Treble Clef

The Musical Alphabet consists of just 7 letters:

A-B-C-D-E-F-G

To read music we must be able to find these notes on the staff. The staff is a system of 5 lines and 4 spaces telling you which notes to play. The symbol to the left is called the Clef. We'll start with the Treble Clef . It tells you what each line and space means, kind of like the key to a map. When music is written in the treble clef, the 5 lines represent these notes:

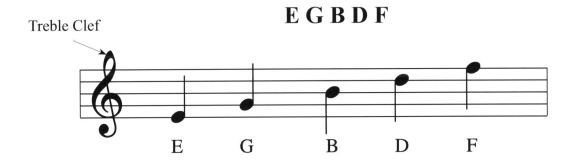

You can remember this by the phrase *Every Good Boy Does Fine*.

The spaces represent the letters:

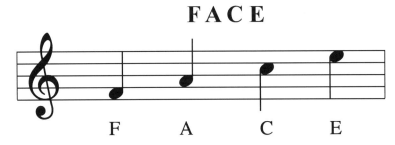

Remember the word FACE. You should memorize these notes and their location on the staff.

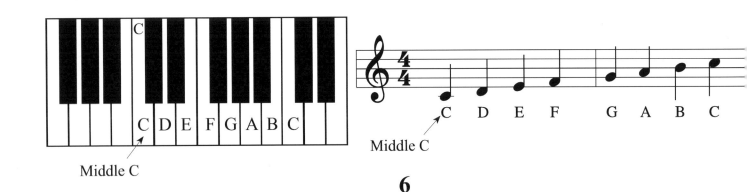

The Bass Clef

The piano uses two clefs, the Treble Clef and the Bass Clef. Generally, the right hand will play the treble clef and the left hand will play the bass clef.

The lines in the bass clef represent the notes G B D F and A. Think *Good Birds Don't Fly Away.*

Bass Clef

The spaces represent A C E and G. Think *All Cows Eat Grass.*

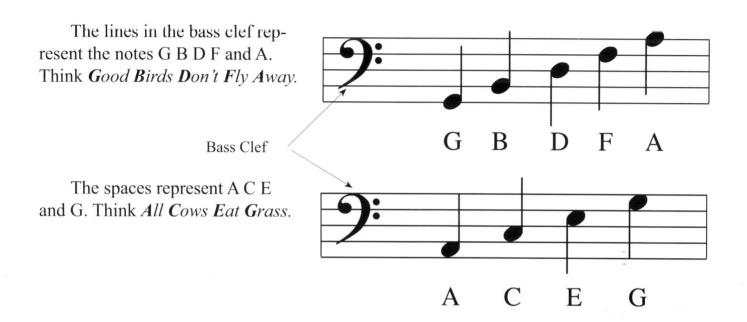

Notes in the Bass Clef

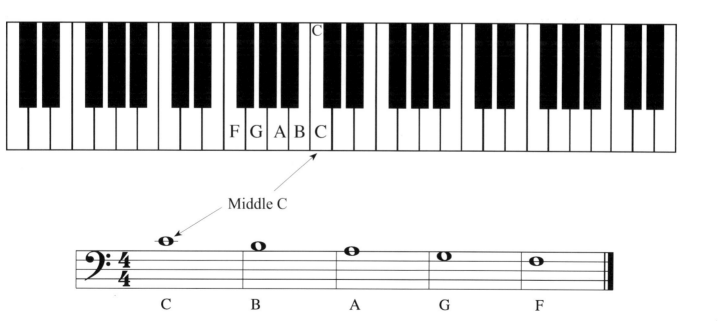

The staff is divided into sections that are called measures. The lines are called bar lines.

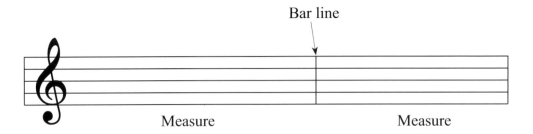

Time Signature

Each measure gets a certain number of counts. We will start with each measure getting 4 counts or beats. Count (1 2 3 4, 1 2 3 4). This is called the time signature and tells us how many beats are in a measure. 4/4 means there are 4 beats to a measure. If it were 3/4, it would mean there are 3 beats to a measure.

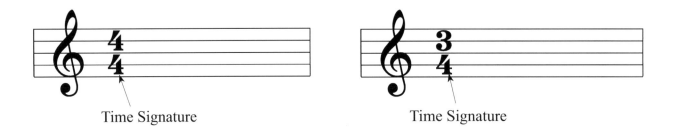

Notes

There are several parts that make up a note: the head, the stem, and with some notes, the flag.

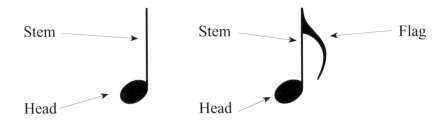

Note Values

Start by learning 3 types of notes, the whole note which lasts 4 beats, the half note which lasts 2 beats, and the quarter note which lasts 1 beat.

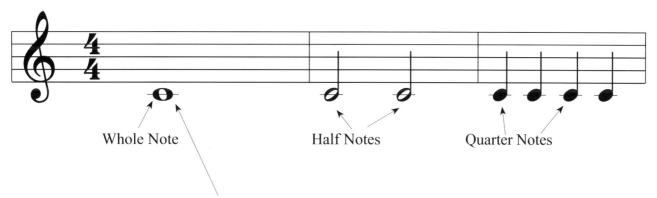

This is where middle C is written on the staff. The line below the staff is called a ledger line, and it allows notes to be written below (and above) the staff.

Rests

Rests are another type of notation you must learn. Rests tell you how many beats <u>not</u> to play. The names of rests correspond to the names of notes. For example, the whole note rest, like the whole note, gets 4 beats.

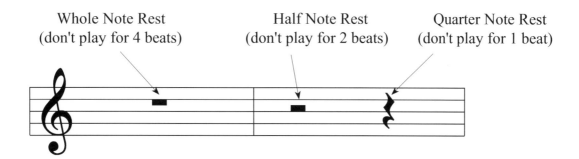

The Grand Staff

Combine the Treble Clef and the Bass Clef to make the Grand Staff. Middle C is located between the two staffs. It may be useful to practice each clef individually, then read both at the same time. Remember to read the notes, not just the fingerings.

= Treble Clef or right hand

= Bass Clef or left hand

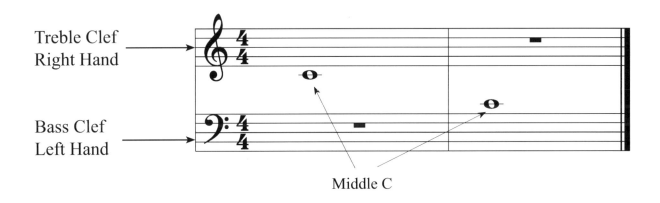

Treble Clef
Right Hand

Bass Clef
Left Hand

Middle C

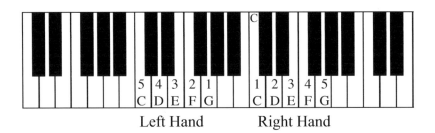

Left Hand   Right Hand

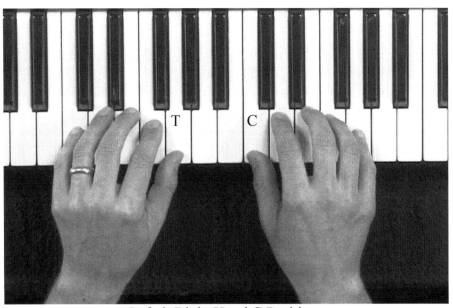

Left & Right Hand C Position

10

Numbering the Fingers

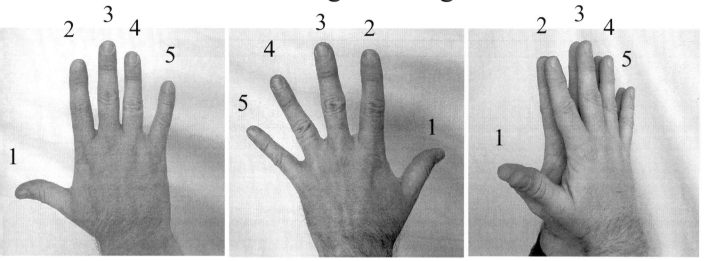

Right Hand   **Left Hand**   **Both Hands**

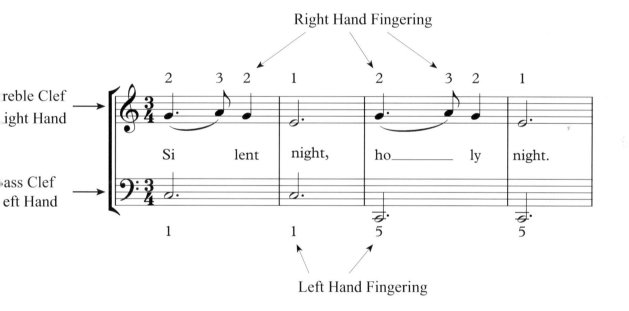

The Songs

Online Audio Access is available at this address on the internet:

cvls.com/extras/egsp

Amazing Grace

Blessed Assurance

Rock of Ages

Nearer My God to Thee

Shall We Gather at the River

Sweet By and By

The Old Rugged Cross

Refrain

21

What a Friend We Have in Jesus

How Great Thou Art

In The Garden

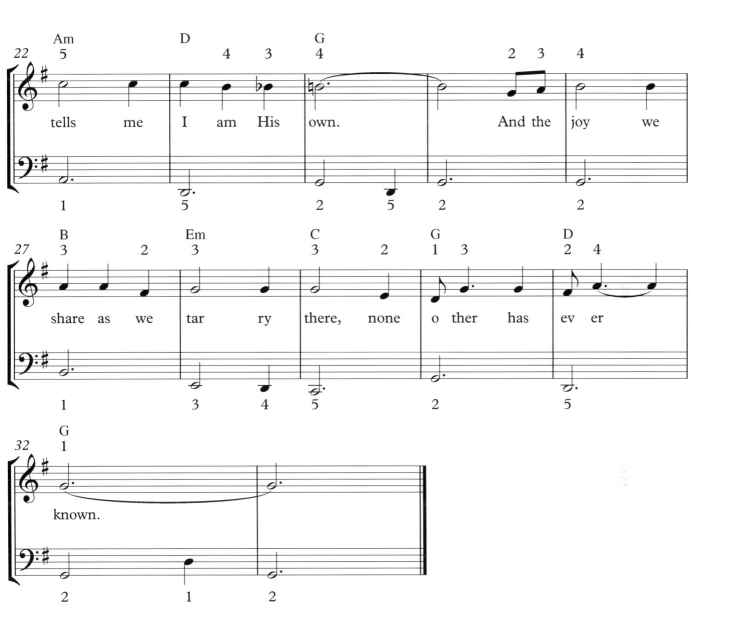

Just a Closer Walk With Thee

Leaning on the Everlasting Arms

Lyrics

This section contains the melody line, lyrics, and chord progressions so that you can play the complete version of the songs with all of the lyrics. This also works great for jam sessions or playing on stage because the lyrics are in a large font with the chord progression on each verse. This section is also arranged in alphabetical order to make finding the songs easier.

Amazing Grace

A - maz - ing Grace how sweet the sound, that saved a wretch like me. I once was lost but now am found. Was blind but now I see

'Twas grace that taught my heart to fear
and grace my fears relieved.
How precious did that grace appear
the hour I first believed

Through many dangers, toils, and snares,
I have already come.
Tis Grace has brought me safe this far,
and grace will lead me home.

When we've been here ten thousand years
Bright shining as the sun
We've no less days to sing God's praise
Than when we first begun

Blessed Assurance

Verse

G   C   G

Bless ed as sur ance, Je sus is mine!   Oh, what a fore

D   A   D   D   G   C

taste of glor y di vine!   Heir of sal va tion, pur chase of

G   G   Am   D   G

God,   Born of His Spir it washed in his blood.

Refrain

D   G   C   G   G   C

This is my sto ry, this is my song.   Prais ing my Sav

G   A   D   D   G   C

ior, all the day long.   This is my sto ry, this is my

G   G   Am   D   G

song   Prais ing my Sav ior all the day long

Perfect submi$\overset{G}{s}$sion, perfe$\overset{C}{c}$t d$\overset{G}{e}$light.
Visions of r$\overset{G}{a}$p$\overset{D}{t}$ure now bu$\overset{A}{r}$st on my $\overset{D}{s}$ight.
Angels desc$\overset{G}{e}$nding bri$\overset{C}{n}$g from ab$\overset{G}{o}$ve
Echoes of m$\overset{Am}{e}$rcy, wh$\overset{D}{i}$spers of lo$\overset{G}{v}$e
Refrain

Perfect submi$\overset{G}{s}$sion, $\overset{C}{a}$ll is at $\overset{G}{r}$est.
I in my S$\overset{G}{a}$vi$\overset{D}{o}$r am h$\overset{A}{a}$ppy and bl$\overset{D}{e}$ssed.
Watching and w$\overset{G}{a}$iting l$\overset{C}{o}$oking ab$\overset{G}{o}$ve.
Filled with His g$\overset{Am}{o}$odness, l$\overset{D}{o}$st in his l$\overset{G}{o}$ve.
Refrain

32

How Great Thou Art

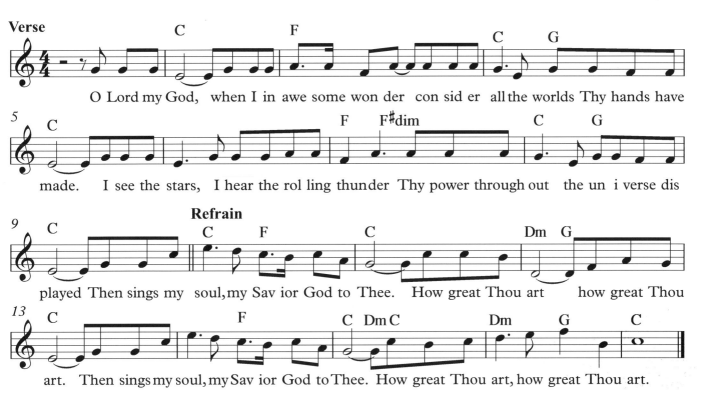

Verse

O Lord my God, when I in awe some won der con sid er all the worlds Thy hands have

made. I see the stars, I hear the rol ling thunder Thy power through out the un i verse dis

Refrain

played Then sings my soul, my Sav ior God to Thee. How great Thou art how great Thou

art. Then sings my soul, my Sav ior God to Thee. How great Thou art, how great Thou art.

And when I think of God, His Son not sparing,
       C   F
Sent Him to die, I scarce can take it in
       C   G   C
That on the Cross, my burden gladly bearing
           C   F   F#dim
He bled and died to take away my sin
        C   G   C
Refrain

When Christ shall come with shout of acclamation
And lead me home, what joy shall fill my heart
Then I shall bow with humble adoration
And then proclaim, my God, how great Thou art
Refrain

When through the woods and forest glades I wander
And hear the birds sing sweetly in the trees
When I look down from lofty mountain grandeur
And hear the brook and feel the gentle breeze
Refrain

In The Garden

He speaks and the sound of His voice
Is so sweet the birds hush their singing,
And the melody that He gave to me
Within my heart is ringing.
Refrain

I'd stay in the garden with him
Though the night around me be falling,
But he bids me go, thru the voice of woe
His voice to me is calling.
Refrain

Just a Closer Walk With Thee

I am weak but thou art strong   Je sus, keep me from all wrong.

I'll be sat is fied as long   As I walk, dear Lord, close er to Thee

Just a clos er walk with Thee   Grant it Je sus, if you please

Dai ly walk ing close to Thee.   Let it be, dear Lord, let it be!

Through this world of toil and snares,
If I falter Lord, who cares?
Who with me my burden shares?
None but Thee, dear Lord, none but Thee.
Refrain

When my feeble life is o'er,
Time for me will be no more.
Guide me gently, safely o'er
To Thy kingdom's shore, to Thy shore.
Refrain

Leaning on the Everlasting Arms

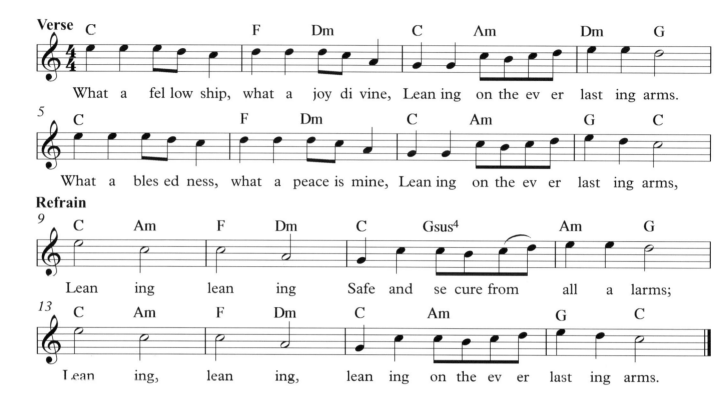

Oh, how sweet to walk in the pilgrim way,
Leaning on the everlasting arms,
Oh, how bright the path grows from day to day,
leaning on the everlasting arms.

Refrain

What have I to dread, what have I to fear,
Leaning on the everlasting arms?
I have blessed peace with my Lord so near,
Leaning on the everlasting arms.

Refrain

Nearer My God to Thee

Near er my God to Thee, Near er to Thee

Even though it be a cross That rais eth me,

still all my song shall be Near er my God to Thee

Near er my God to Thee, Near er to Thee.

Though like the wanderer, the sun goes down
Darkness be over me, my rest a stone
Yet in my dreams I'd be nearer my God to Thee
Nearer my God to Thee, Nearer to Thee

There let the way appear, steps unto heav'n
All that Thou sendest me, in mercy given
Angels to beckon me Nearer my God to Thee,
Nearer My God to Thee, Nearer to Thee

Then with my waking thoughts, Bright with Thy praise
Out of my stony griefs, Bethel I'll raise
So by my woes to be Nearer my God to Thee
Nearer my God to thee, Nearer to Thee

Or if, on joyful wing cleaving the sky
sun, moon, and stars forgot, upward I fly
still all my song shall be nearer, my God, to thee
nearer, my God, to thee, nearer to thee!

Rock of Ages

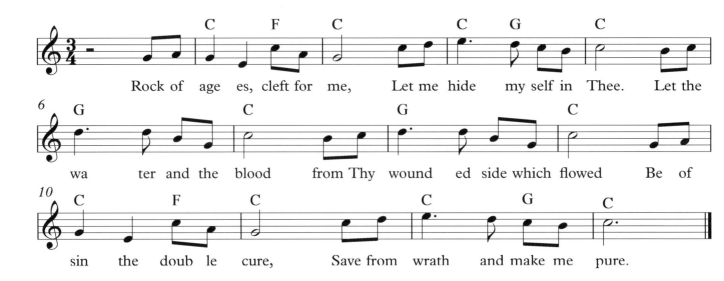

Rock of age es, cleft for me, Let me hide my self in Thee. Let the wa ter and the blood from Thy wound ed side which flowed Be of sin the doub le cure, Save from wrath and make me pure.

Not the labors of my hands
Can fulfill thy law's demands
Could my zeal no respite know
Could my tears forever flow
All for sin could not atone
Thou must save and thou alone

While I draw the fleeting breath
When my eyes shall close in death.
When I rise to worlds unknown
And behold Thee on Thy throne
Rock of Ages cleft for me
Let me hide myself in Thee

Nothing in my hand I bring,
Simply to the cross I cling
Naked, come to thee for dress
Helpless, look to thee for grace
Foul, I to the fountain fly
Wash me, Savior, or I die

Shall We Gather at the River

Verse

Shall we gather at the river, where bright angel feet have trod

With its crystal tide forever flowing by the throne of God

Refrain

Yes, we'll gather at the river, the beautiful the beautiful river,

Gather with the saints at the river that flows by the throne of God.

On the margin of the river,
Washing up its silver spray,
We will talk and worship ever,
All the happy golden day.
Refrain

Ere we reach the shining river,
Lay we every burden down,
Grace our spirits will deliver,
And provide a robe and crown.
Refrain

Soon we'll reach the shining river
Soon our pilgrimage will cease,
Soon our happy hearts will quiver
With the melody of peace.
Refrain

Sweet By and By

We shall sing on that beautiful shore
The melodious songs of the blessed
And our spirits shall sorrow no more,
Not a sigh for the blessings of rest
Refrain

To our bountiful Father above
We will offer our tribute of praise.
For the glorious gift of His love
And the blessings that hallow our days
Refrain

The Old Rugged Cross

O that old rugged cross, so despised by the world,
Has a wondrous attraction for me,
For the dear Lamb of God left his glory above
to bear it to dark Calvary.
Refrain

In that old rugged cross, stained with blood so divine,
A wondrous beauty I see,
For 'twas on that old cross Jesus suffered and died,
To pardon and sanctify me.
Refrain

To that old rugged cross I will ever be true,
Its shame and reproach gladly bear,
Then he'll call me some day to my home far away,
Where his glory forever I'll share.
Refrain

What a Friend We Have in Jesus

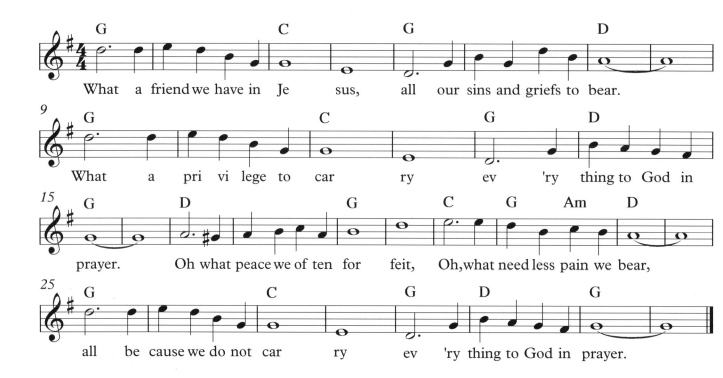

What a friend we have in Je sus, all our sins and griefs to bear.
What a pri vi lege to car ry ev 'ry thing to God in
prayer. Oh what peace we of ten for feit, Oh, what need less pain we bear,
all be cause we do not car ry ev 'ry thing to God in prayer.

Have we trials and temptations? Is there trouble anywhere?
We should never be discouraged, take it to the Lord in prayer.
Can we find a friend so faithful, who will all our sorrows share?
Jesus knows our every weakness, take it to the Lord in prayer.

Are we weak and heavy laden, cumbered with a load of care?
Precious Savior, still our refuge, take it to the Lord in prayer.
Do they friends despise, forsake thee? Take it to the Lord in prayer.
In his arms He'll take and shield thee, thou will find a solace there.

Companion Gospel Books

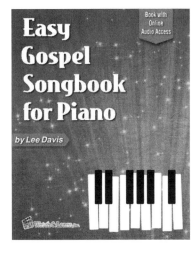 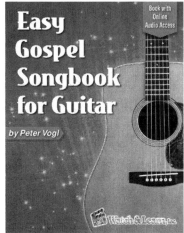 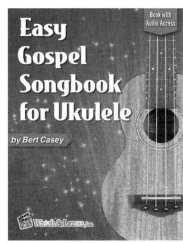

Companion Hymns Books

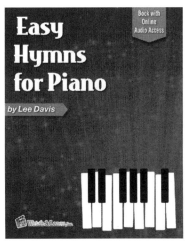 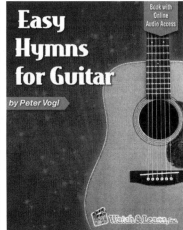 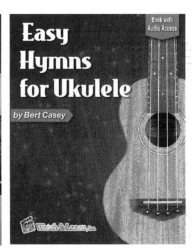

Companion Christmas Books

 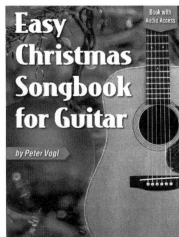 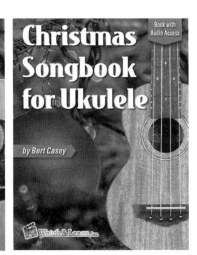

These products are available on Amazon.com. If you have any questions, problems, or comments, please contact us at:

Watch & Learn, Inc.
2947 East Point St.
East Point, GA 30344
800-416-7088
sales@cvls.com

Printed in Great Britain
by Amazon

69070132R00025